PEP TALKS FOR

Catechists

ENCOURAGEMENT,

SUPPORT,

GUIDANCE

JANET SCHAEFFLER, OP

TWENTY
THIRD *23rd*
PUBLICATIONS
www.23rdpublications.com

Twenty-Third Publications,
A Division of Bayard; One Montauk Avenue, Suite 200;
New London, CT 06320; (860) 437-3012 or (800) 321-0411;
www.23rdpublications.com

ISBN: 978-1-62785-103-9

Copyright ©2015 Janet Schaeffler. All rights reserved.
No part of this publication may be reproduced in any
manner without prior written permission of the publisher.
Write to the Permissions Editor.

Printed in the U.S.A.

Introduction

Some days, everything in our lives runs on track. Our responsibilities and relationships are in sync and effortless and we feel as if we can tackle anything. Other days, everything seems to fall apart. We end up discouraged and demoralized. Such times call for words of encouragement and support. They call for a spiritual pep talk.

Are there times when you feel like that as a catechist? One day, everything is going smoothly, effortlessly, and with a feeling of accomplishment. The next day, you find yourself questioning, discouraged, overwhelmed, or worried.

Jesus says to each of us, "Come to me, you who labor and are weary..." (Matthew 11:28). On our dark days, our frustrating days, Jesus welcomes us, in all our tiredness and hesitations. On those days, we depend on each other, we support each other, we encourage each other, and we point out to each other all the good that we might sometimes miss.

During your prayerful moments amid the discouraging times, may these reflections of guidance, insight, and vision remind you of who you are, whose you are, and the sacred ministry to which you are called.

Contents

Why did I say yes? We're about to begin, and it seems so overwhelming!

God continually says to us, "I have called you by name: you are mine" (Isaiah 43:1). Within God's constant, affirming call, there is always an invitation to use our gifts for others.

Even though the invitation to be a catechist might come through another person (our DRE, pastor, a friend, etc.), the invitation ultimately comes from God. We aren't merely "helping Father" or "assisting the DRE"; we have been distinctly called by God because of our baptism, because of our gifts.

As we begin this year—and even throughout the months and years ahead—we might wonder why we said yes. Are we really competent enough to do this? There's a saying that reminds us that "God doesn't call the qualified; God qualifies the called."

Because this is a call, a vocation, when we do our part (taking part in our ongoing formation, developing our catechetical skills, and building love and respect for the learners), we know we are doing God's work. God is saying to us, "You are the one I need. You are the one who will make a difference. I know you, and I have chosen you." Responding to that call from God, we use our gifts and our committed faith for the good of others.

TO DO » Remember these words: "God who began this work in you will carry it on to completion" (PHILIPPIANS 1:6).

TO PRAY » *Inviting God, deepen in me your call. Strengthen me to do your work.*

1

I don't know the parents and families of those to whom I'm ministering!

Faith does not grow and develop in isolation; the faith of each one of us (and especially of children and youth) is impacted by all we are, all we do, and all the people in our lives. For children and youth, the most constant and enduring influence is their parents and families.

So be creative and intentional to get to know the parents and families of your children and youth. Knowing them—having a relationship with them—will help you in designing your sessions and in choosing examples to use. The families and children will be touched by the personal interest you show in them.

Before the year begins, call the parents to introduce yourself. Ask what you can do for them. Ask for their ideas on how you can work alongside them as together you surround their child with a faith-filled environment. Respond to the families throughout the year, especially to any happenings you hear about: births, illnesses, special achievements, deaths.

TO DO » Make a plan to call or e-mail each parent (perhaps one family each week) to give a compliment about their child, sharing something considerate the child has done or a trait/virtue you have witnessed in them.

TO PRAY » *God of all families, bless the families with whom and to whom I will be ministering during this year. As you protect and care for them, empower me to be a faith-filled witness, a sign of your love for them.*

It's difficult to bring God to people. How could I ever do that?

You're right: it is difficult. But the reality is, that is not our job. We don't bring God to people. God is already and always there. Our role is to invite people to slow down. Our role is to help surround them with experiences in which they become more aware of how God is already in their lives.

Even though we are engaged in catechesis, which is different from education, the definition of "education" is not "to put in," but "to draw out." All catechesis (and true education) is the drawing out from the learner of what is already there. Catechists encourage and enable the learner to notice God, who is already there.

As catechists, of course, we need to pay attention to our experiences of God in order to walk with others and guide them to recognize their ways of experiencing God. We might have different experiences, but it's who we are—and how we live our relationship with God—that influences others. For instance, people might not care (or get excited) about the history of various forms of prayer within our tradition, but they'll listen when we share how prayer has sustained us, or the various types of prayer that are meaningful in our own lives.

TO DO » Who has walked with you, guiding you in new awarenesses of God in your life? Thank them today.

TO PRAY » *Ever-present God, lead me in this catechetical journey with so many others. Help me to be a witness and guide.*

I don't think anything got accomplished today.

Sometimes, after a session, we feel that all we did was struggle for their attention or attend to problems. "Some days are like that," remarks Alexander in *Alexander and the Terrible, Horrible, No Good, Very Bad Day.*

Perhaps the question is: how did we respond? Often the things we do, and how we do them, teach a great deal! In the midst of these "some days," our challenge is to remain peacefully centered in God and to be kind and considerate as we call the youngsters to the "more"—the more of respectful behavior and participation.

The *General Directory for Catechesis* reminds us that nothing—not the method or the texts or any other part of the program—is more important than the person of the catechist (no. 156).

Sometimes after a session, we might feel that "the content" of the lesson plan didn't get across; amid all the distractions, there wasn't sufficient time to explore it. Yet what *did* happen? How did we respond? Did our faithfulness to God, our respect for each person, our desire for the best for each learner, our peace-filled demeanor, and our commitment to learning and growing in our faith journey "teach" the children and/or youth?

TO DO » When you're away from these "some days" for a little bit of time, reflect on—and give thanks for—all the blessings that did happen on these days.

TO PRAY » *God of interruptions, increase in me your way of responding, of leading, and of caring.*

But I'm not creative!

That depends on what you mean by creativity. Often, especially as catechists, we think of creativity as "doing arts and crafts." But that's not our role. When we do use artistic expression—and we should—it's for the purpose of helping others delve deeper into meanings and to express for themselves—in their unique way—their understanding of the connection between faith and life.

What is creativity? God made us human, gifting us with creativity. All people have the capacity to be creative.

Steve Jobs said, "Creativity is just connecting things. When you ask creative people how they did something, they feel a little guilty because they didn't really do it; they just saw something. It seemed obvious to them after a while. That's because they were able to connect experiences they've had and synthesize new things." That's what catechists do: we connect faith and everyday life.

The famous cellist Yo-Yo Ma said, "Passion is one great force that unleashes creativity, because if you're passionate about something, then you're more willing to take risks." That's what motivates catechists: passion in their love for God and in their desire to share it.

TO DO » As you plan your sessions, ask yourself: Do the activities allow for the imagination, the dreaming, the wondering, the response of each learner? Or do I expect the end result to be the way I want it?

TO PRAY » *God of creativity, inspire me and guide me so that I may see enthusiastically with new eyes, and so that I may connect your love to all I'm called to do.*

Something seems to be missing. What really should I be doing?

My one-year-old great-niece was enjoying lunch so much that, after each spoonful, she said, "More, more!" Is there something about our catechetical process that inspires the call for "more, more!"?

The "more, more!" is that our faith touches all of life. What really should we be doing in every gathering time? Touching the head, the heart, and the hands. Faith formation is about knowing something, being something, and doing something.

Sometimes, because of time, we might stop with the head. We share all the facts and beliefs. They are important! Yet even in knowing all that is needed, the real questions are: What difference does it make? Who am I? What am I called to do?

In touching the heart, we experience that we are called to be friends with God, that God calls us to an intimate friendship that touches who I am and all I'm called to be and do.

In touching the head and heart, formation and life overflow to our hands: our desire and call to do something. To be disciples is to do what Jesus did—and what Jesus would do today in our world.

TO DO » Check your plans for next week. How are you touching the heads, the hearts, and the hands of your learners?

TO PRAY » *God of all life, guide me as your message molds our heads, our hearts, and our hands—to know you, to love you, and to be your presence in our world.*

I don't think it's working.
I don't see any results!

n life, we often want to see immediate results. But immediate results don't happen often in the formation of a person's faith. Building relationships (with the children and their families) that will encourage faith formation does not yield spreadsheet-friendly outcomes.

We know in our hearts that faith formation is a lifelong process, but how often do we expect the children to grasp it all right now? How often do we expect to witness immediate, transforming changes in attitudes and actions?

We probably will never know the full effect of our ministry. It's what St. Paul tells us (1 Corinthians 3:6): "I planted the seed, Apollos watered it, but God has been making it grow."

TO DO » Keep a journal, writing down all the good things that happen (during your sessions and with interactions with the children and families outside of the program), even the little things that you might forget after a couple weeks. Remember the challenges too. Rereading your journal several months later will probably recall to your mind and heart all the things that did work, that made a difference, and that were God-moments of growth.

TO PRAY » *Waiting God, you are never impatient with the time it takes for growth, for conversion, for discipleship. Help me to carefully plant and water the seeds, always trusting that it is you who are making them grow.*

It's December. I'm so busy with other things, and their minds are elsewhere.

What if we focused on thinking of and living this reality in a different way? Even in the midst of the busyness around us—and all the things we *really* have to do—it's the season of Advent, rather than the season of frenzied activity.

The church invites us to celebrate Advent for many reasons: to slow down, to live in the silence and stillness, to appreciate anew the gift of God becoming one of us, and to ask ourselves questions (how do we wait in all the happenings of our lives? how do we prepare and watch for God's constant coming?).

Take a deep breath each day (perhaps more than once a day). Live in the moment of Advent, cherishing its many meanings of preparing ourselves to live deeper lives with our God, who lives among us and loves us unconditionally. Talk with your learners about what this means for them as you meet during your Advent sessions. Most of all, live Advent serenely and joyously. Your attitudes and actions will not only deepen the calm in your life; they will be a model for the youngsters as well.

TO DO » What one thing could you do today to slow down and enjoy the Advent season rather than rushing around? What could you do to make your Advent sessions peacefully filled with God's stillness?

TO PRAY » *God-Emmanuel, God-with-us, teach me the ways of living simply and peacefully, even if the world is rushing around me.*

8

I don't know all the answers.
Why did I say yes?

A bishop new to his diocese visited the oldest priest in the diocese and asked him, "What has helped you to stay faithful in ministry for so many years?" Without hesitation, the old priest replied, "Well…I knew someone who knew someone who knew someone who knew someone who knew someone who knew someone who knew someone who knew Jesus."

Who you are is most important. Your relationship with Jesus is most important. Because you know Jesus, you will make a difference in the lives of your young people. As we pass on the faith (at home and at the parish), more is caught than taught.

It's not that "knowing our faith" isn't extremely important; we always have an imperative responsibility to continue our learning and growing. At the same time, all the preparation and study in the world will never give us all the answers to every question (and that's exciting, for there is always more to learn). It's all right to say, "I'm not sure, but I'll find out, and we'll talk more about it next week." Encourage your learners too to do research and to talk to their parents and grandparents to find the answer.

TO DO » Enroll in a class, participate in a parish or diocesan workshop, or read a book to deepen your understanding of the faith.

TO PRAY » *God of mystery, open my eyes, my ears, and my heart to learn more deeply and to teach more earnestly.*

What are the parents doing at home?

Our call as catechists includes much more than relating to the youngsters whom we meet each week (or each day). Our ministry is to the whole family. We do expect that the parents will follow up our catechetical sessions at home by praying together and being involved in care and service of others. Our role, however, is not only to have these expectations but to support, encourage, and empower these parents in their vital role.

Our expectations (and how we share them) are significant. Research and experience tell us that what we expect is usually what we get. If we expect families to be faith-filled (and we affirm them for all the ways they are), they will most often respond.

Our support, encouragement, and empowerment are crucial. Often parents want to pray at home, and they want to talk about and live their faith with their children, but they're not sure where to begin. Each week, why not mail, send home with the children, or e-mail a short and practical suggestion for prayer, a conversation starter, and an act of service?

TO DO » Once in a while, snail mail a note to each child, complimenting them and sharing how glad you are to have them in your group. Thank and affirm the parents—in notes to them, in the Sunday bulletin, and even in the local paper.

TO PRAY » *God of great expectations, show me how to expect and to affirm, how to assume and to support, how to imagine and to encourage.*

I'm lost! I don't know what to do about...

This is not a lone-ranger ministry; we're never alone!

In some languages, the translation of "catechist" is "to grab a hand and walk along with." That's certainly referring to those to whom we're ministering; at the same time, it reminds us that we're never alone. First, of course, God is with us. Prayerful reflection often brings insights and clear ideas about our questions, situations, and things to do (or not do).

Never be afraid to ask for help. Because we are created by God to be a community, there's much help around! That's the role of your DRE; she or he is always ready to help. Ask another catechist (who has taught for a while) to be your mentor. Contact someone from a neighboring church or a friend in another city. Take part in one (or more) of the numerous webinars that are available for catechists.

Rely on the catechists with whom you're teaching. If possible, go early and meet over coffee to share ideas. Keep a book on the table where you meet so that you can jot down prayer intentions, remembering each other in prayer.

TO DO » When you need help, ask for it. When you're having success and when something is going right, offer to help someone else.

TO PRAY » *Helping God, thank you for your constant presence, for providing insights, and for lending support and encouragement. Thank you for the many people with whom you surround me whose hands I can grab and walk along with.*

Why did I say yes?
At times I have questions and doubts.

Being immersed in teaching—and understanding our faith more deeply—can bring questions, sometimes even doubts. It might even seem like a loss of faith, but in reality, it is the opposite: growth in faith. In *Leadership Is an Art*, Max De Pree reminds us that growth comes only through living with the questions.

Take a moment to remind yourself that we are not meant to, nor will we ever, fully understand the mystery of God. St. Thomas Aquinas said, "If you have understood, it is not God." Karl Rahner, a theologian of the twentieth century, reminded us, "If you are talking about God and you think you know what you are talking about, you're a heretic." Thomas Merton prayed, "If I imagine You, I am mistaken. If I understand You, I am deluded. If I am conscious and certain I know You, I am crazy."

Questions are normal—and good. They lead to the ongoing journey of deepening our relationship with God. Our experience of asking questions also helps us understand the continuous questioning and wondering of today's youth. We walk with them on the journey.

TO DO » Search out someone with whom you can share faith and your questions and wonderings: your spouse or good friend, your DRE, your pastor, or a parishioner whom you admire.

TO PRAY » *God of the questions, as I search for answers, remind me that the search is the journey, one that will always keep me connected to you.*

We're halfway through.
I feel in a slump.

T he sun might not be shining; it might be very cold; we're back to "ordinary time"; everything seems kind of boring. January can be a big slump time both in our everyday lives and in our catechetical ministry.

One human tendency is to see everything in life as a series of things to get through; there's an exciting beginning, but then we're always waiting to reach the end. Hence, the "middle" can be tedious and tiresome. What if we saw things as God does? What if we saw that everything is a new beginning and that this present moment is spectacular and filled with possibilities?

The "middle" can be a time of assessment, bringing to mind all the good things that are happening: What is my goal as a catechist? How has my prayer changed? What have the children responded to most enthusiastically?

The "middle" can be a time of change and new approaches: Is there a new way to pray during our sessions? Could we try a new activity? Is there an opportunity to invite a guest speaker? Are there unique ways to invite the learners to take responsibility within our sessions?

TO DO » Do one thing differently within your sessions: change the seating; use more music and drama; ask more "what if" questions; use technology for learning and prayer.

***

TO PRAY » *God of the middle times, open my senses and my imagination to all the new promises lurking in every corner of my world, especially in the learning times with my youngsters and their families.*

Sometimes I just don't understand. They seem to live in a different world!

That can be very true. Children (like all of us, really) hear everything that we, or our books, videos, and materials, say through their own generational filter.

Jesus talked about the good soil. The *General Directory for Catechesis* begins with his parable of the seed falling on good soil. Throughout the Directory, the bishops remind us of the necessity of always remembering the field in which the seed is sown—the everyday lives and experiences of those with whom we walk on the journey of faith.

Spend some time frequently listening to the music, watching the TV shows and movies, surfing the Internet, and paying attention to the books and trends of the age group to whom you're ministering. Attempt to "walk in their shoes." Try to imagine what life is like for them.

One thing that connects us—no matter which generation we live in—is the beauty and truth of our Catholic story. Within your sessions, connect this faith story to their life stories. Continually invite them to conversations about their life experiences—and how they are connected and lived out within the Catholic story.

TO DO » Outside of your session time, talk with someone in the age group to whom you are ministering. Ask them about their questions, their likes, their joys, and their worries.

TO PRAY » *God of all, continue to open my eyes and heart to see the beauty and potential in each unique person.*

They just don't seem to be interested.

Like all of us, children and youth have many "pulls" in their lives, many things on their minds, and many things to do. Amid all this, inviting them to zeal for their faith and for our faith formation sessions can be a daunting task. Perhaps one approach is to stop "doing church" to our learners and invite them into "being the church" of God. People often say that youth are the church of tomorrow. In all that Pope Francis has said about— and to—today's youth, he illustrates that they are the church of today. Treating them as important members of the church, inviting them to responsibility, to active involvement, and to service, will spark their interest.

Perhaps too, today's youngsters are not being challenged. Faith formation requires meeting the needs of the age level we're working with, but the content, the practices, and the life applications do not need to be watered down for anyone. Challenge your learners to think—to truly reflect—outside the box. Challenge them to act boldly. Jesus said, "You will do the works that I do, and greater works than I have done" (John 14:12).

TO DO » Call one of your learners (and/or their parents). Ask them for one or two ideas that they think will spark the interest for everyone during future sessions.

TO PRAY » *Enthusiastic God, ignite in my heart wholehearted awareness of you and eager faithfulness to you. Let these spill over in all I do with your young learners.*

I'm discouraged.
They're not in church on Sunday.

Often we might hear our youngsters say, "We don't go to Mass on Sunday." This challenges us to a precarious balance: to not respond in judgment while, at the same time, sharing with them the importance of—and the gifts that come from—celebrating Sunday liturgy with the community.

Often, of course, the decision to participate in Sunday liturgy is not the child's; we don't want to make them responsible for something that is out of their control.

They might not be at liturgy, but they are with us each week. Often it takes only one significant person to be an enthusiastic, faith-filled model—and nudger—in a child's life. Catechists can be that person. When we speak often of the privilege and joy of worshiping together, of God's invitation to the table, of the comfort and challenge of Sunday liturgy, we are planting seeds. When we use liturgical rituals during our sessions (the sign of peace, the sign of the cross on our forehead, lips, and heart before the gospel) and link them to liturgy, we are planting seeds for participation.

TO DO » Send an e-mail to your youngsters' families, suggesting things to watch for in the coming weekend liturgy (a line from the readings, a general intercession for the parish's First Communicants, etc.).

TO PRAY » *Faithful God, you call us together for prayer and worship. Deepen that desire, that gift of unity in Eucharist, in each one of us.*

Everything is happening all at once in my life. I don't have time for this!

There are days (probably too many of them!) when the myriad responsibilities, obligations, and concerns of everyday life seem to be crushing and engulfing us. The feeling can be: I just want to quit everything!

These times do call us to step back and to slow down—to take time to reflect and more deeply understand all that we're doing. Why are we doing these things? What are our priorities? What is most important? We're reminded that the main thing is to keep the main thing the main thing. With that awareness, where do we want to give our time?

At the same time, in order to be realistic and balanced, we periodically need to take time to reflect upon our commitments. Are there ones that

- we could say no to?
- don't bring life and joy?
- we're called to do because of our gifts, because of all we've been given?
- we would like more time for?
- could be shared?
- could be given away (to someone eager to help)?
- make a difference in the lives of others?

TO DO » Take time to name all the positive reasons you spend time as a catechist.

TO PRAY » *God of all time, slow me down. Help me to recognize you in all my commitments.*

I don't know enough about this week's topic.

Perhaps it would be true to say, "We never will." One of the enlivening realities about our faith is that there will always be more to learn, more to appreciate, more to celebrate, and more to act on. One of the gifts of being a catechist is that a journey of study and deepened understanding is inherent in what we do as we prepare and as we listen to the insights of others—all those on the journey with us, especially the often-provocative thoughts of the children.

At the same time, there might be times when we do feel that "this week's topic is beyond me or confusing to me."

I recall observing my two-year-old great-nephew watching *Who Wants to be a Millionaire?* As soon as a question was asked, he delighted in responding, "Phone a friend," "Ask the audience," or "50-50."

We too have many lifelines. Rely on your DRE, other catechists, your mentor, and the various resources from our Catholic publishers. Invite someone to your session who has expertise/experience with the topic. As a permanent fix, look, with your DRE, for a co-catechist so that two of you will minister together, each doing parts of the session that call forth your gifts.

TO DO » Take time for prayer before preparing each session. Read, participate in adult formation sessions, and keep a list of those to whom you can go for assistance.

TO PRAY » *God of guidance, teach me your wisdom. Be my lifeline.*

Some people are "difficult." What can I do?

Yes, there will be times when children (and parents) are disrespectful, unkind to each other, uncooperative…the list could go on. Perhaps our first response should be to change our focus and to try always to see others as God sees them. Rather than seeing them as "difficult people," perhaps we can see them as people made in God's image who sometimes are difficult, hurtful, or stubborn.

Another approach is to remember the often-quoted catchphrase "act as if." What if—in any of these situations—we acted as if we saw the kindness in the person, the respect of which they are capable, and the cooperation they are ready to give? How might children (and others) respond when they are treated as loved, exceptional, and incomparable people?

Our attitude and actions in any of these situations are key; in us the children (and others) experience the voice, the hands, the heart of Christ.

At the same time, of course, as the leader within the catechetical sessions, we set the environment of cooperation and kindness from the very beginning by naming—with the children—the guidelines and rules for respectful behavior within our setting.

TO DO » Whenever there is a difficult situation, spend time in prayer for the person involved. Recall one of the ways they show their goodness, and compliment them on it.

TO PRAY » *God who sees beyond, you see the goodness of each person while always calling us to the more. Let me see with your accepting eyes.*

The year is over.
I'm not sure I made any difference.
Should I do this again?

Have you ever heard an adult say that "nothing happened" in the religious education sessions of their youth, but then, at some later point, faith became a priority for them? What prepared them for this new urgency? All those years when they (and probably their catechists) thought nothing was happening, the foundation was being laid.

Years ago, Cardinal John Dearden (in a homily written by Bishop Ken Untener, and often mistakenly attributed to Archbishop Oscar Romero) shared these words of wisdom: "We plant seeds that one day will grow. We water seeds already planted, knowing that they hold future promise...We cannot do everything and there is a sense of liberation in realizing that. This enables us to do something, and to do it very well. It may be incomplete, but it is a beginning, a step along the way, an opportunity for God's grace to enter and do the rest. We may never see the end results, but that is the difference between the master builder and the worker. We are workers, not master builders; ministers, not messiahs."

TO DO » Return to the journal you began earlier this year. Prayerfully talk—and listen—to God about all the "somethings" you did paving the way "for God's grace to do the rest." Is God calling you to continue next year?

TO PRAY » *Ever-faithful God, thank you for your unceasing actions in my life and the lives of the children and their families—even the ones I cannot (yet) see.*